'Haskell's poetry, so often set in familiar environments and concerned with the day today 'realities' of life, is in fact ... a consideration of what the poetic voice means in the "real world".' *John Kinsella, Southerly*

'Issues of gender and the domestic, and movement through (or against) perceived masculine and feminine spaces are beautifully and sensitively observed and managed – an uncommon thing in male Australian verse.' *John Kinsella, Southerly*

'Haskell's poems appear in many forms. Rather than nurturing a single way of speaking, Haskell adopts various shapes and tones and allows each poem its own evolution ... Incidental rhymes and semi-formal sound patterns are offered with considerable subtlety and persuasion.'
Kristen Lang

'Haskell's shaping of language is highly skilful ... the language is heightened just that notch at the appropriate moment ... for the poetry to singe the reader's senses, jolt the mind or open a new window of perception on to the world.' *Rod Moran*

Haskell's poetry 'demonstrates how human the art of poetry can be; how it can deal with the particulars and universals of our emotions and remind us of our commonalities'.
Geoff Page

'Mundane and ethereal, ordinary and extraordinary merge into images that stir us to a new consciousness of life lived today ... registering a continuity and a modernity, evoking in us a paradoxical sensation and perception of the evanescence and the solidity.' *Subas Chandra Saha*

Dennis Haskell is the author of seven collections of poetry published in Australia, the Philippines and the UK, and author or editor of fourteen volumes of literary scholarship and criticism. He was co-editor of *Westerly* magazine from 1985–2009 and is currently a member of the Management Committee of the Westerly Centre, and a Senior Honorary Research Fellow at The University of Western Australia. Haskell was chair of the Literature Board of the Australia Council for the Arts from 2009–2011 and is currently Chair of the Board of writingWA. He is the recipient of the Western Australia Premier's Prize for Poetry, the A. A. Phillips Prize for a distinguished contribution to Australian Literature, and an honorary doctorate of letters from UWA. In 2015 he was made a Member of the Order of Australia. Dennis Haskell has served as visiting poet and professor at universities in England, France, Germany, Italy, Singapore, Thailand, the Philippines and the USA.

Ahead of Us

DENNIS HASKELL

FREMANTLE PRESS

The things we shrink from are the things we make poetry out of.
Peter Porter

… all that we love will escape us sooner or later, and
we cling to it as if it should endure eternally.
Jean-Jacques Rousseau

i.m. Rhonda Haskell (1947–2012)

CONTENTS

CHANCE

CHANCE: A CONVERSATION

Chance, I know that my chances
of having a conversation with you
are slight, at the very best, I
know it's no use taking exception
to your presence, but what on earth
are you doing in this life? Your place
seems so arbitrary; and
if we could sit down together
I know the talk would be hopelessly

haphazard, since love could lead swiftly to gardens to garbage,
a line of poetry might read
"kohl adrift more she role ti dah".
There are those sure your heart belongs to Dada
but you know its heart belongs to you.
So around the world we'd go on a
marvellous, maddening, richly frustrating excursion
in which go is only occasionally distinguishable from woe.

Some think you are not the ultimate
in godliness, which you find a glorious test;
you who know no meaning know meaning best.
Only when we get to death, in
which you see you have a role, we part company.
You say, "In the end that's the subject
which is for you, but is not for me".

NEVER

The surreal numbers flicker like
eyelids, 100 kph, 150, 200,
the nitrogen-filled tyres now
more skittering than turning, whistling
to the ground like a fingertip touch
at parting, 250, then suddenly
we are clear out of this world,
its scattered lights that had stood
above us at intersections, tending fragile
corners, lonely doors, now patterned
crazings on a glazed painting. Cézanne
was correct – there are only two
dimensions: them and us. And here,
above life, there is nothing
we would wish never end
but the never of ending.

THE GIFT

Small clouds flock outside the window
like phlegm in the sky's throat
that we fly into, hoarser and hoarser,
the engines coughing above cut outs
of paddy fields, deep olive green
plantations intersected by water,
and dry strips of land, where men
and women work: nature is being
put in its place. Lower and lower

until we are being whispered about
by destiny, or chance. We hang
dangling at speed, in fragile air;
but today luck chooses us, the
headlines will escape our names, we will enter
the miraculous serenity of procedures,
of routines, all our fear buckled up
in a gift of banality, of schedules
that even we will quickly forget;

then the rumble and crack of wheels
on the ground, hooked by gravity and
weighty again. The most valuable
elements of our lives are hardly noticed.
Now the sun's gleaming off the wings
and we're heading homeward in the light
at last unperturbed by its luminous
and utterly ordinary silence.

FRENCH POEMS:
LA CATHÉDRALE NOTRE DAME

What would Our Lady, or anyone's, think
as uncaring crowds swarm past
her buttresses, and flashbulb lights
far outnumber the flights
of prayers? An amplified male alto
soars like a linnet through the Gothic aisles,
unquestionably glorious. Stone everywhere as if
to keep the earth out. A brilliant father offers
confession in French, English, Italian, Japanese.

Jean Verdier, Jean Juvénal des Urse sleep
secure in their improbable faith, in
this belief museum, amidst circular
candelabras of devotion, their
deepest 'truth' barely flickering. Yet
uncertainty is a kind of grief. The cameras assert
a dearth of ideas. People exit, troop off
to the awful Tower. Bones seem stronger
than belief, yet they also rot in earth.

REMEMBERING JEAN MOULIN

Remembering the scarf-necked, firm
and almost smiling face of Jean Moulin,
I looked at the statuesque,
almost imperial Arc de Triomphe,
turned and walked with a few
thousand other hurrying, dawdling,
window-gazing, free and fanciful faces
along the vision-wide boulevarde, the
expansive paths of the Champs Élysées:
feet and cars and motorscooters,
and dead, wet leaves; Peugeot, Swatch,
Louis Vuitton tout en or, Lacoste
beside Fouquet's grand brasserie,
Galeries des Champs and the Galerie des Arcades,
Sephora's infinite rows of cosmétiques,
Les Comptoirs de Paris, while Yves
Rocher offered nature for a price,
a literary collection mentioned
"Les Écrivains et la Mélancolie".
Whatever's wrong with them
Club Méditerranée will take you away
from the Mediterranean, the paradisal fields,
the peck-peck-pecking green-necked pigeons
where your purse or wallet speaks
its triumphant Esperanto, and
lights are strung out in the trees.

[Jean Moulin was leader of the French Resistance during World War II]

AFTER ROISSY

Having endured what no-one could call
a good night's sleep, not half a night
but at least some, I lumbered towards Liège
on a slow country train. More sleep
than you, My Love, would have had
after quitting Roissy Airport,
Paris glittering far below,

and I calculated the minutes when
you must have stumbled
off the plane, and gone straggling
through Changi, your head
tired, your eyes struggling open,
ankles swollen, your legs
enjoying being legs again, the
muscles stretching, the blood
starting to flow freely. Outside,
a chimney belching great
gouts of smoke, as from
an old train, white cows
head down in lush grass,
a potholed track down which
two women push infants, ragged
clothes strung out on a ragged line.

When you stepped behind
those slicing doors, reality
simply walked away. So I sit here and yet
step along Changi's carpeted floors,

past the resplendent orchid displays,
past shining perfume shops,
past iPod and CD players, beckoning
like insinuations of happiness.

Time goes on
no matter what we do or say,
and from my window
the twisting roads, the
crooked-back farmhouse roofs,
the cigarette-chimneyed towns,
and the long, flat fields
of Belgium
stretch far away.

THE TREES

It is a cloudy day when the light
does not seem ours by right
but only borrowed, and all time looks
much later than it deserves to be.
The land leans out of the window
at your elbow towards where a sunrise
of thought, of ideas, of understanding
should be. Trees mark out distances
like goals, and there are more of them
than your mind, or the light,
can hold. What are they doing there
to you? What are you doing here
racing through the uncontrolled landscape
of your life, all the stations
that will be given to you?
Near clouds clot the air and early
darkness is closing in like fear.

CHINA POEMS:
POEM BEGINNING WITH A LINE BY LI PO

"Our floating life is like a dream ..."
In 1775 Shen Fu, about Yün, their lives
already entwined: "I asked for the manuscripts
of her poems and found that they
consisted mainly of couplets and three
or four lines, being unfinished ... I wrote playfully
on the label of this book ... and did not realise
that in this case lay the cause
of her short life." Beginning
Six Chapters of a Floating Life.

Tianjin, Beijing, Shanghai, Nanjing ladies and men
by tens of thousands on tens of thousands
of bicycles, mopeds, motorscooters, motorbikes,
gauze their faces, handkerchief their mouths,
so many particles of dust and lead
pixel the air. The clouds ache, then
mud and uncertainty pour onto streets
while the wind swings its shrill seizures
all around my windows, nature's opera
makes an immediate audience of millions.

And pausing over Shen Fu and Yün,
their lives afloat, I think
of our single lives, of last year, when
death almost swept you away.
In Hangzhou, Ferrari, Versace, Louis Vuitton
arc the magnificent West Lake,
obelisks of apartments arrow the ground

like headstones for the living.
As far as anyone's eye can see
the small, ancient villages are being swept

into the prim nostalgia of history. Now
stinky tofu in the streets, Starbucks,
azaleas in flower, a traffic soldier's shrill
whistle – ignored – the rush of feet
fills the street, and the next street, and the next, and the …
Dodging battalions of legs, on pedals, flat to floors,
coming from a three-quarters empty country
the faces come toward me, staring straight ahead,
too many to think the "What if?"
of other possibilities.
I find it hard to believe in

individuality, that each gaze has
in mind fears, whispers, expectations;
Chinese count in numbers so enormous
they add up to anonymity.
No matter how many faces you see
there are always more, no matter
how many arms and hands you touch
there are always more, no matter
how many motorbikes and voices you hear
there are always more …

And beginning here without you My Love,
surrounded, drenched in this dense, teeming life,
I feel as if the world itself were short of breath,
floating,
and all China a stretch of long silence.

AT THE MARCO POLO HOTEL

When Marco Polo went to Hangzhou, long ago,
he had beauty and bewilderment to go;
now he can rest in a hotel that tourism feeds:
it is especially designed to meet you all needs.

Located in the luggage desk, we provide you with
the service of transportation and savings for free.
We are not responsible for any loss or damage
while you are check-out. If you are stolen
call the police.

Satellite TV channels are available for details.
Please refer to your TV program.
The water from the gap in the bathroom
can not be drunk directly.

Café Le Mediterranean – It is located on the
17th floor. To enjoy the best beautiful
panoramic view of West Lake while
savouring typical local tidbits,
this is a real life.

Each floor equipped with modern Fire Prevention
System, Please does not move casually
except emergency.
Civilization does not reach for the sky,
neither do we.

No encounters with members
of the opposite sexes in the rooms that
is what the lobbys is for.
Guests are invited
to take advantage of the chamber maid.

Be prepared for danger
in times of safety.
We have only one earth, just like
we have only one pair of eyes.

And at every turning, then and now,
Marco's and your eyes
meet mischievous surprise.

TAPPING

My Love, that odd window knocking
you no doubt remember
I never heard
"till there was you"

is simply the tapping
of yellow-beaked Singapore birds
as they fly from scrawny cats.

I hear it nightly, that tapping
sharp in the air. You've gone and

all I hear now is clear and spare
as if everything stood outside me.

Sentimental Beatles songs I play
soar over flurries of cats and birds

– you once said the wish
to recapture youth, to tumble over
the cliff face of the past

"is the first sign of senility".
In Singapore's absurd, befogging heat

I want desperately to write you
a poem of the scrawniest simplicity

to tap and beak inside you,
flown into a language
full beyond words

from the flurry of my feelings,
from the pit of my life
where I am now,
as dumb as the animals.

INSTINCTS

for Ann Jamieson, wherever she may be

One day, one summer, about 1959
my mate and I approached tall,
long-haired, pony-tailed Ann Jamieson
with a cacophony of bugs and beetles
we must have taken days to collect.
She shrieked, and fled in terror,
we chased, aiming at her hair
hysterical locusts and bewildered beetles,
delighted with our bravado,
her schoolbag flapping on her hips.

This apology comes late by fifty years.
Boys who have reached eleven or twelve
have odd ways of showing they like you
which girls who have reached eleven or twelve
strangely, find difficult to construe.
We laughed like larrikins,
unaware of the urges which had lain
so long in the chrysalis of our bodies
and had now begun to stir and buzz.

NATURE AND THE HUMAN

I spent a week at St Anne's-on-the-Sea
For a dose of English summer – wind and rain mainly –
But I never did manage to see the sea.

I stayed at Breverton, the lovely B&B
Where Anna and her kids were kind as kind can be:
I spent a week at St Anne's-on-the-Sea.

I looked far, as far as any eye could see
And saw sand flats stretched across the estuary
But I never did manage to see the sea.

The tide crept in at night, oblivious to me
Through the force of nature's perversity
I spent a week at St Anne's-on-the-Sea.

Fish and chips and a pint – a gourmet's specialty;
Under "No dogs" signs dogs walked nonchalantly
But I never did manage to see the sea.

I thought nature and humans could readily agree
But the sand flats leached away endlessly:
I spent a week at St Anne's-on-the-Sea
But I never did manage to see the sea.

WORDS WITHOUT LIMITS

Our lives are granted us,
gratuitously. Out of a huge and unfamiliar silence
first breaths
thump into our bodies. More
than our minds could ever collect
is there
and with us always. Call it "God".

On a morning
in summer
just before dawn
the earth collects herself and all her relations,
awaiting her eyes' opening
onto a permanent dialogue of light.
Our veins might flood our bodies
merely to be part of that sight.

Why then this infernal questioning?
Living there and
always being what we are,
what is there
is what we never want to leave.
Always leaving it, calling to it,
we are always expecting it to jump
out of our own eyes.
Confusing our minds with the wind
we blow in our own contradictions.

The wind thumps against our bodies;
breath stiffens against the wind;
the skin tightens around our teeth:
reminders that we creep
back into that absence of ourselves,
the moment that waits for us with hands apart
like an insistent host

who demands defection
from every thought, each desire. So
what can we construct
in "living",
this constant struggle for affection?
Coarse habits of expectancy,
the thump of contradictory hopes,
a collection of compromises,
a life,

this flooding of our bodies?
What can we make of those hands, that expectancy?
A silence that allows
all possibilities. Call it
"God".

NO-ONE EVER FOUND YOU

No-one ever found you self-seeking or dishonest.
Giving is your gift. When you stand
on the spotted tiles, peeler in hand,
large-eyed, intent
on pontiacs, carrots and all the care
for yet another meal, you think yourself
ordinary, like the magpies
that march about outside the windows
while the afternoon light
drifts across geraniums, daisies, lawn,
but nothing and no-one could be more distinct.
Living never came easily to you. You take everything hard.
All that we have ever said and done

seems less than what we meant
but to know this without saying
is love's bequest, the silent embodiment
that gives our every word its meaning.
We have shifted cities, our shift
into each other's lives so complete
that any other we could scarcely know.
Though your eyes are tired, my shoulders bony,
it matters little where we go,
how little we know
and how much our lives have passed,
our days will be filled with green
and we grow together like the grass.

THE CALL
for Kieren

A stifled room to which I am called
by an unknown voice, not knowing,
because of its great stillness,
that it calls from my son's sleep.
In the bush nothing stirs. For once
no breeze grabs hold of the curtains.
Sunk back into his body the voice quietens.
I shift his legs, twisted in the sheets,
grateful that this sudden nightmare
has crept back into its own beginnings.
In his sleep I can hold his arms or arrange his breathing
without objection,
his will gone, sleep
like the end of an illness.

How we look for meaning in such actions,
as if God's voice called from the centre of our sleep,
but there is nothing: only a silence so complete
love itself might become a sickness.
What we inherit from the bush is a need for voices:
myself calling to my son in his recurrent silence.

So I listen again for his voice, or someone's: nothing
but silence come on us as it eventually must
and the need for sound greater than the need for any thing.
"God" is a word sunk deep in the blood, signifying
the certainty
silence will one day flood our arteries,

the hope for some voice, come
prowling through our sleep.

Over the tips of the trees, out across the face of the ocean,
nothing moves.
It is a humid January night with no breeze.
His body is in my hands.

THE BASIS OF ALL KNOWLEDGE
for Cameron

He is a child
less than three feet tall, impotent,
his fingers not yet curled
around problems.
He screams with pain
for the simple fact that
his teeth bite his gums like needles.
Take him up.
He has no beliefs.
He displays no regret
nor any knowledge
of what regret could mean.
He entrusts you and
your meaningless arms
with his whole body,
with nothing less
than his whole life.
Take up what will not be questioned:
a father given to his son.

WASHING THE DISHES

Not long after we met,
our early 20s,
we laughed through Europe
in winter. Little cash,
ate bread and jam dinners
in the shuddering snow
and huddled
on the criss-crossing trains,
slept in their clacketty warmth.
Deprivation never bothered us:
we could rough it and
we had all the vivacious curiosity
of the young
and I would have sworn
we were in love.

Over 15 years ago
one child was born, then two.
You had a cruel time
of their coming. How many
hours of crying close to laughter
and laughing close to tears?
And now out of the asthma-
racked uncertainties of childhood
we have seen them grow
almost beyond us.
They surely were, and are,
the manifestation of love

which dares be slops and suds
once romance has riffled
through a pairing of lives
its dazzling, fragile laughter.

NIGHTS OF AVERAGE NERVES

Well, possums …

An evening of soft, nonchalant cloud
when a thin breeze, flexible as rumours,
lifts off autumn branches, leaves
as thin as eyelashes, above
scratchy, orange-ribbed rooftops,
wires twisted tight to the poles
and the lights they enable
awake in the living rooms.
Water meters tick like crickets,
wheels roar a moment outside each door
and then are away. Everywhere is aware
of somewhere else.

Somewhere else. As though life here were surplus,
measured out by remote urges to purchase.
Lines are strung out in realistic,
dun-coloured backyards
where simple, complicated lives
are pegged out to dry
and enter the time scale of dreams;
there deep waters run still.

Across all the television-greyed,
junk-mailed, ineffectual dog
barking in a yard, ragged
roses, milk carton suburbs
intellectuals spread contempt

as black as Vegemite, read reticence
as simplicity, repetition as monotony,
caution as selfishness,
as if average nerves never shared
the ludicrous intimacy of pain,
or joy hovering on the ridiculous,
as if they had no past, a sunshine
where no shadow of thought
could ever dare fall.

Gazing above the trees, they miss it all.

ON NOT FLYING
a reply to Kit Kelen

The noise never stops wherever you are.
It spins feverish inside your head
with the gravity of the world,
its whirled obligations, roles, responsibilities.
Above the world you are taken into time
that is wholly relative. Here on the ground
it's absolute, and absolutely resolute.
It determines our days. It hands out
our jobs, like a teacher at school.
It gives us this day's demands, and
forgives no trespasses. Just do it!
Starting now. It gives us everything but itself.

And so I stay silent to friends, miserably silent
to getting ink on paper. We lay waste
our powers. I respond to emails, obey the phone,
take my seat at the worn committees, give seminars,
give classes, edit a journal, wipe the desk of papers,
stack the desk with papers, talk my head off
for what is, with irony, called "a living".
Parsons once had those. Ink fixed on paper
will never be the world, the richness we recall.
We fly hardest who don't take off at all.

AN ACT OF DEFIANCE

It's as if he turned with a grin
and a wave, then disappeared
behind a door irrevocably
marked "No Entry"
and took off into air
where we, stuck to
the earth, can't follow.
Already his presence
is falling out of us
like dust. He is gone,
gone out of our eyes,
the feeling of him
gone from the tips
of our fingers,
the scent of his presence
evaporating from our hazardous
hearts. Now the wind blows
flat along the branches,
the sun lies
like desolation on
the burnt out grass.

Now the world is emptied
of time. Now
we must tread through the days
with heavier attachments.
Picking up the pen
is like picking up a stone.
Life is a game in which

we are all given
the role of losers
eventually. But each attempt
at meaning is an act
of defiance of death.
So he turns, smiles and waves
in my mind again
as though we had
all the time in the world.

ON THE VERGE
for Kieren

The older you get
the more small things matter.

Get washing sorted, the dishes
stacked, the ironing board out,
plants watered, roses clipped,
the old table clumsily restained,
the junk dissected;
it's suburban clean-up time
and on each street's verge
half the stuff of our lives
awaits collection.
In Adelaide, radio reports of Australia
bowled out again, in Israel fires, the eastern wheatbelt
licked by floods, WA's
dusted in drought.

After, on the tip of the dark,
sitting alone at the café,
an unseasonable breeze
and surprising rain
skim the tables;
young people laugh past
to the bars, the restaurants, voices
tipsy and frisky
with anticipation, to them
the flimsy rain doesn't exist.

A drab, nothing day in a way.

But this evening one call from my son
in Taiwan, to say he'll be away
for five days – he wants me to know –
and all the small, mundane world
and everything it holds
suddenly sings its vivacious,
gracious, lighthearted mystery.

TINNITUS

5,000 angels dance on a pin
creating a thin, high-pitched singing
in the empty area of my ear,
plucking each high harp string
in a Morse of ping and whistle;
I can hear the whistle
but can't discern the music,
suffer its relentless din – day
into stinging night into day.
It can't be cured the doctors say
so they play audiologists' tricks
to fool my brain. My curative sound's
the shilly-shallying of surf,
of water fussing and trembling
on sandy shores, or flopping
a susurrus over rocks. You can hear froth
laced to the surfaces of sound.

For a year I've listened
to this slumbrous rustling cure,
surf splashed in the computer's core,
gushed through the car's soft speakers,
water thrushed over my head
in whispering sleep.
And still the angels sing
their dog whistle tingling,
their unchanging I Ching,
the shrill denizens of my inner ear.
A thousand pins drop tinkling

down cliffs of ice, and zing
again in a tympani of feeling;
for folly is as folly does:
this brain is not for fooling.

CONSTANCY

I stared out on the midnight streets
of Canberra, so still they looked
frozen in time. The nearby
clock tower was stuck
at a quarter to eight, early
even by my blood and bones
like a wish that we
would never age,
from this instant. Canberra:
it's what Australians like
to say about it – out of time
and stuck in a world of no
human's making. To be alive
is to be moving
away from where we are,
even in sleep. And I thought
of you, as I always do, the better
part of me, far and yet near,
in a two hours different space.

This one constancy, as still
as a winter street telling me,
in a way that catches my breath,
that time is only a window
I could climb through
and touch you, in life, in death.

THE EDGE OF AIR

23 November 1973,
twelve o'clock in the muddy streets,
wind hits each shoe with slush
as I pick my way through restless Lewisham

imagining Francis Webb, an embattled believer
who picked his way through words
until the Word, the Word made Flesh, the Star of Holiness,
stuck like a thorn in the side of despair,
illumined his journey, moistened
with the communication of God.
He bothered me with his Catholic certainty,
the way he held it to the finish,
to the last chokings in the eerie sounds of death.

Now he travels on the edge of air
his words hover on silence; romantically
I imagine him there, elevated, beyond despair,
angels' fists battering his hair,
his feet shifting through "Heaven"
as if that could satisfy
what we are on earth,
his words the traces of a journey
where the truth is as necessary as ever.
Might I believe he died with words
like "God" dry on his lips?

Now I could wish his silence climb
beyond the edge of silence, beyond lies,

while words huddle around our edges,
and the edgy, unsatisfiable
night swallows my footsteps.

HOW CLOSE TO CALLIGRAPHY
for Robert Gray

Through the graffitied windows
of a rackety Sydney train
I look out on "hectares" of suburbs
but the word sounds odd to someone
who grew up in feet and inches, and still
thinks ordinarily of acres, who remembers
"chains" and "roods" and "perches",
those useless imperial words
now mummified in bandages of silence

utterly unlike the silence of margins
– not the so fashionably academic
outside the suburbs,
but that white space
at the ends of our lines
that publishers insist
readers insist on,
the spaces that show we believe
there is always more to be said
and readers might say
or at least might think it.

Now, when every year seems an extra,
a parody of the death that
has already silenced my father, I've somehow
come to think that 'God' is the least
likely to say anything,
and be very calm about

that clear-as-a-wardrobe silence.
Why should the years make me meet
His or Her blankness with tranquillity
when those same years have taught
that the wisdom I once thought
we'd grow into
is as distant as a beacon in hell?
So here on the wrong side of 60, with fewer
years to come than have already been,
on a train sliding quickly
through Sydney suburbs
I can see hundreds of kids, and their
screaming parents, all with European,
Arabic or Asian faces, scramble across
huddled fields, and hundreds of girls
scamper down lines, lean up to netball rings
with avaricious anticipation. Life is
up there and out there. Later, at the Quay

ferries ruffle back and forth beside
and underneath the black arched bridge.
What would Slessor have made
of the Quay's didgeridoos,
the jugglers, the tourist throng
– let alone drunken Joe Lynch?
I meet a poet friend, slightly older than me
for talk and late dim sum lunch.
He met Slessor once, who told him
"Get a haircut!" Good friends, we talk
and talk where St Mary's bells
crenellate the air. But how long before

it's not just bells and chopstick clicks
that punctuate our silences?

THE DAY DOROTHY PORTER DIED

We rarely met in recent years, except perhaps
in print, which meant you meant to me
always youth. You were still at school
those Sunday mornings we flitted across
the black steeled Bridge and glittering Harbour
to Zika Nester and the Ensemble's acting classes
in the wildly full-of-promise 1960s. You learnt
more Method than I ever did. We were
not actors but writers – and I somehow
knew it then. Full of animation, you were
young and short and smiling, and your voice
grew through poetic lines
unlike any other voice I ever knew.

Skip a decade, and we met again
with the *New Poetry* crew
now long since dissipated – some of them
dissipated then – you did act
the Little Hoodlum you never were
as if that was poetry too; instead
you were still young and short and smiling.
Undergrad years are years of hope,
dreaming spires or not,
and we had Brennan's
but largely apart – you were leaving
as I arrived. Time
seems to only gently slope
away from youth, until
you're in its plummeting gash of earth. Still

a Poetry Society where *honi soit*
qui mal y pense
knotted us on a fragile rope
of separated words.
After that just a scatter of meetings,
different cities, as the years twisted past.

***

At the office, compulsory reading, administrivia,
I checked a postgrad's thesis
nearing its end, answered sundry requests,
handled papers, emails … Then you were on the news
in the worst possible way.
The day I heard you'd died
we struggled to find parking where
my wife met her curmudgeonly oncologist
who, mercifully, gave her a good report,
we watched over my cousin, starring
in a hospital named "Hollywood"
where he lay minus
his cancer-filled prostate, I telephoned
the widow of a friend
whose cancerous lungs gave out
years ago – what is this curse
that moves among us so silently?
Breast cancer
stalked you like an arcane, dogged
beast from those mythological and historical
stories you loved. For Christ's sake
what's *its* method?

All day your death was a wall
I had to get over or through,
we lay waste all the gettings and comings,
those of us who could enjoy
the unpredictable luxury of breath,
passing again and again, as you couldn't,
through the Checkpoint Charlie of death.

AHEAD OF US

In the black crow and owl hours
when consciousness should be
stricken with rest,
swift iron groans, inaccessible,
incomprehensible fright
jerk our thoughts half-upright.

Freight trains speak their barely understood language
in and out of deafening silence,
each turn of the wheel a syllable on the line.
We think of them as clambering wrongly
out of the night
but they belong; the spreading blackness is theirs
by right – we who semi-conscious
hear their wheel rumbling and high-pitch horn
as dim, barely understood
shudderings and shrieks
are mere eavesdroppers on darkness.

Freight trains moan on the line.
What does their shaky language spell
and carry? What is its urgent load?
What refuses to dissolve,
its tongue determinedly calling us
into the determined dark?

THAT OTHER COUNTRY

The poetry is in the pity.
Wilfred Owen

THAT OTHER COUNTRY

The skies of your life are unerringly blue
and you have no plans to rearrange
your expectations; but when the licensed official
says the word, you, and those
closest to you, immediately shift
to another country. No matter that
you do not seem to move, and others
do not recognise your departure, you
are now in exile. The word
will be a visa, in your passport
an indelible stamp, and your passport
now full of pages that you will never use.

There are no tense allegations:
your arrival is an application
for permanent residence, approved
without question;
your questions do not matter.
The government of that country
is entirely different. We know
that we will all die
but here your friends live each day
in the expectation of life. Now
you will live each day, each hour, each
minute in the expectation of death.
In that country there is no capital planning,
no budgeting, no small talk, no migration queues,
no day to day distraction
from the dictatorship of death. Forget

the life of the mind, although the citizenry
is full of meaning. Where everyone is a refugee
the body asserts its supremacy, the economy
is measured out in medicines and pain.
You will wonder that there is no system of justice,
the only wars are within you,
the UN convention signatures are
all missing, yet ethics and care are everywhere.
There gravity pins you to the earth
more tightly; the very air can be exhausting.
Move slowly in this place
if you must move
where the noisiest sound is silence.
There is no resisting the journey
or putting it aside – later, later …

No use to declare
stark ignorance of the language.
He says the word, "cancer",
and already you are there.

EVENTUALLY

The Big C
is coming to visit you
and coming to visit me.
It's not if but when
he'll stiffen in the doorway
blocking out all the light.
Your lack of invitation
will not deter his right
never to go away:
once he's here
he's here to stay.

All other subjects will become him.
He will teach your only thought
is not your only speech.
The immensity of his smile
will command your every breath,
while his metallic taste
fills your mouth,
his demeanour, his nausea
coats your teeth.
No fibre of you will escape
his claustrophobic intensity.

The intense Greek derision
of lusting body by steady soul
will make more and more sense.
All Logic, Hope, Justice
he will condense, into Luck.

Fuck those long thoughts
of your soul; his very howls
will ensure you are
a prisoner of your bowels.

You may become so attached
to him that life will prove
a poise of loneliness,
his speech a long silence
the true measure of noise,
with an idiotic,
metaphysical sense of glee.
The Big C will ask us
why are we in this carcass
whose acts prove so reckless,
that it can't be who we are!
The Big C
is coming to visit you
and coming to visit me
eventually.

AFTER CHEMO

Your hair is falling like thin rain,
like mizzle, like long, silent,
lightening snow. An invisible waterfall,
your hair cascades
or lifts away from you
like gossamer, like an inkbrush
gifting new patterns to the floors,
furring our mouths, our thickening thoughts,
our almost-said words.

In each corner of each room,
swirled across the tiles,
I find them, these networks,
these fine cobwebs of you;
they're flowering down your clothes:
every jumper, every skirt,
even your socks are
laced with these filaments,
hair like slender moths,
like will-o'-the-wisp,
these fine threads of you,
drifting away ...

And our lives are fastened
by more shadows
than we cast.
Your hair
lisps like autumn blossom,
aspects of the you

you used to be
on racks in the wardrobe,
alert in the trembling air.
Just outside the bedcovers,
the you you were, seeming intact

but in fact
we are as we are
together, alone, as you can see,
with elusive memories for company,
with your wisps of hair
disappearing as gently as breath.

DRINKING

I strike a match, bash
the light switch off
and, candle flickering,
drop into another century
when thought was slower:
I need its pace,
this slowing of the mind,

as another mug of tea
you've asked for
but been unable to drink
is swallowed by the sink

and I lean silently
over the benchtops
swallowing hard

while the tea
gurgles and gargles
in the sink's
metallic throat.

YOUR SHADOW

Now you share your every action
with your insistent twin;
with a fraction of your effort
it tracks our whims and our griefs
though it is my shadow
only vicariously.
Whatever you do
it is unerringly you
but less than you;
so it and I have developed
a humbling relation
about what it will do
and it will do and it will do.

Your shadow
is your uncanny dancing partner,
wherever you lead it follows.
Whatever the time of day,
no matter that clouds sway
across the entire sky,
it concertinas the stairs,
slants over your chair:
its grimness is a kind of solace
that nothing else needs attention.

Your shadow
being cast from inside you
lies beside you
even in the night;

sometimes it seems to glow
with a special darkness;
sometimes it is so strong
that I seem to cast it too.
Persistent as a god,
its natural state
is nothingness.

Your shadow
will concentrate our minds
until it stretches
in protracted stealth
and becomes more you
than you yourself.

WHO OR WHY OR HOW OR WHAT

I was so used to the nausea, the anguish,
the stomach pains, your stumbling,
arm aided walk, the diarrhoetic dashes, the slow
sleepless nights, your arms shuddering,
pinpricked like a junkie's

that when the preoccupied secretary
hurried to us, split open the thin-lipped
envelope, and briskly explicated
the intricate scientific
phrases as "all clear",

I wept, and couldn't accept it,
and I wondered, as the two words sank in,
who or why or how or what
had catapulted our lives away
and just as blithely decided
to fling them back. So that now
everything could seem the same as it was

except that the waiting room, the chairs,
the sky outside, our hands, your
turbaned wisps of withered hair,

were all new, entirely.

ON THE EVE
Wednesday 18 May 2011

My dearest darling Rhond, I write this to you, or me, or to space on the eve of yet another operation, but I need to write for the horrors and anxieties – probably paranoia – that overtake me in the long, dark reaches of the night – hours when every element of imagination is an ogre. I imagine having to ring our boys, your father, your sister, my mum, everyone, to say the operation has gone horribly wrong. I imagine the surgeon, someone with him to provide support – support him, not me – while he tells me the hardest part of his job is not slicing apart flesh – your flesh – or reaching and tearing out organs – but this impossible sitting down to say, unaccountably something went wrong, the risk was small, but there was a chance, a .5% chance of dying on the table. Unaccountably …

He is still wearing his gloves and gown, half-human – he will go away to be haunted by this forever, but not as much as me, as us. Then a moment of sense jumps up and says this is ridiculous! But immediately I am back in an alternative horror – you've lost too much blood, the anaesthetist has misjudged the dose, the cancer cells are everywhere like children in a playground, your body couldn't take it. It's five years of this battling disease, rising and sinking against its strength or temporary weakness, building and building – a tsunami that pushes aside or surges over the flimsy dykes of reason, and again I am, we are, swimming, floundering, drowning in a hysteria of worry so unlike the impassive, unthinking march of cancer and all the science the surgeon gets to fight it.

Tomorrow he will do the job, and both our lives hinge on the steadiness of his hands, and his impersonal skill. It is no match for our emotions. One day, we know, we will lose this battle – the body and all its absurdities always wins. Until then we struggle, and fight, and sinfully almost pray.

BELIEF

You never see him move
but now he sits silent
in the expectant corner
of every room you enter.
It is his appalling serenity
that hurtles you
into lip-bitten anger.
Though he stares ahead
as blank as eternity
his eyes never leave you,
toast your anger into melancholy,
melancholy into the concession,
the bathos of self-pity. Injustice
finds you everywhere. You can declare
that this is your room,
your house, trespassing
will not be tolerated
but he knows who is trespassing
on your useless proclamations
and will never forgive them.
His silence is the future of noise,
his poise the futile end
of restless striving. Arriving
in each room you
may close your eyes
and resolutely say you do
not believe in death.

But, true or untrue, death
will never
not believe in you.

SO MUCH COURAGE

We sat in the oncologist's
neat, magazine-free room, where
sometimes I find myself
sitting still,
while he in his deadpan
manner – matter of fact voice
and no movement of hands –
offered mild chemo (mild
because the stronger had already
rotted your kidneys)
which might not work
or the delicately named
to hide its brutality
"palliative care", and said
with an unexpected gentleness,
"Don't decide now". As I sat there
I knew you would choose
an avenue, dark, nameless, without end.

You would have no more
of the barely restrained
hair-desiccating, gut-shucking
horror of chemo.
You were calm
as if *we* were leaving you
yet I was fighting furies
I dare not show.
You said it was worse
for me than you:
I never believed it.

So we flew to Sydney
and said goodbye to family
one by one; you offered each woman
– your sister, my sister, my brothers'
partners, my mother – your few pieces
of jewellery, your worldly goods,
and spoke to each with a thud
of quiet finality

while I stood beside you
too terrified to open my mouth.
So much courage
as if you held a sheath
of repressed lightning
that ripped through me, through us,
while I stood
truly pathetic and dumb
and shook, ravished
from head to foot.

RENEWAL

Your driver's licence
renewal notice
arrives in the post
innocently enough
– after all, it's just
a notice,
part of the trivial,
pay-attention-to-this,
administrative detail
of our lives.

You must choose:
one more year or five.
"Just one",
you say, playing
the Scotsman's daughter,
"I wouldn't want
to waste the money";

and something funny
folds up
inside me
and keeps trembling
its flimsy, papery breath.

PLATO'S ERROR

Cabbage moths, white
like torn pieces of skin,
flit in and out of the garden beds
eating what vegetable
leaves they need.

Your skin, thinned out like paper,
itches constantly, and you scratch
like a dog with fleas.
It's the medicines they say.
Medicines designed not to cure
but to endure, to keep
the cancer at bay
a little longer. For five years
our lives have orbited illness
and for six months now
have been sucked
into its light-defiant
vacuum.
Your skin slumps on
the mannequin framework of your bones.
On the few occasions I hug you
I have to do so oh so gently
it barely feels like touch.

Misery attends us. Our friends
are frightened to call,
understandably. I must remind myself
that silence is a form of consideration.

Shadows slip through
slats in the outdoor chairs;
from an angle of sunshine
they look more real
than the chairs themselves
(Plato got it wrong)
as real as skin
fluttering, peeling its way
out of our lives.

SIX YEARS

Outside, streetlights shine
like low slivers of moon
and people move
energetically about their lives.
For six years
we have slipped
into the black pit
of illness and death
again and again,
climbed out
with no suggestions of doubt

then slipped back
and climbed out
again and again.
You cry in the shower
at your wasted, hairless body,
your now small breasts
sagging like two
unanswerable questions,
and I listen, hidden beyond the door
helpless, useless.

It is exhausting.

Why you are tired
I know, poison
surging through your veins.
"Why am I so tired?"

I ask the air, frustrated,
then realise
always, coming and going
to doctors, chemists, hospitals,
arriving and leaving,
sifting through all the medicines to take,
all the things to do,
whatever I do, whatever I think,
the unstoppable core of me

is already grieving.

PARALLELS AND ANTITHESES

Walking near home I stop
at the old railway crossing
and stare down those
endless iron tracks,
their distances shining
even on a cloudy day.

Years ago I wrote a poem
that ended with railway tracks
as "the longest footprints in the snow".
It was in America, Florida
– would you believe Melbourne Beach? –
in deep summer actually:
poetry's world is separate
though deeply connected
to reality. I was thinking
of two girls who picked me up
and put me up, this odd
Australian hitchhiker. I remember
retying their bikini tops.

Later they dropped me at a college,
organised one student to take me in.
He thought I had fucked them both
and couldn't believe my luck. I let him.
Actually they were more lovely than that
but this was 1971. The roads were free
and everybody was a hippy
or wanted to be
or was too frightened to be.

Now cancer has you in its grasp
again – by the lungs,
by the ovaries, by the spleen
– what in Christ's name
does it matter where!
Soon you will be gone
and I know I will stare
down those endless tracks
that once seemed to lead somewhere,
that now lead nowhere,
and think it
a worthwhile place to go.

SATURDAY NIGHT AND SUNDAY MORNING

1.

The end, in the end, came quickly
and astonished us all. Now
it sits like a great, still
stone weighted inside
my pitiful heart. When I think
of it my breath whoops,
catches, every number adds
to zero, every thing
sinks inside my being.

2.

On Thursday you were ill
but not unusually so; you still
cooked dinner determinedly – elaborate
seafood crepes I thought delicious.
You didn't; you ate a bit
determinedly, and shuffled to bed.
On Friday you were ill,
nothing new. At night
you would not eat, except
for some of an egg I boiled, and bread.
You could reach bed early,

but first I tried to ring
our younger son; it was
his birthday. Miraculously
he had just finished his shift
and was free. Your talk was good

and short; you smiled.
It kept you up
a little while longer.
Coincidentally
our older son who never rings
on Friday night called from Taiwan
– business was slow.
And you talked.
I asked was it the best part
of the day, and you smiled
a huge, broad
words unnecessary smile.

On Saturday you were ill.
I was to go out early
though I didn't want it,
but you insisted,
strong enough
to firmly protest.
When I came home
you were asleep. I'd never known
this before. I wrote a note,
then went to the shops. I had a fantasy
about coming home to find you
had died in bed,
but I dismissed it as ridiculous,
as yet another
of the thousand fantasies I've had
over the last almost six years.
When I came home again,
you were still asleep.

I checked – nervously – but it was sleep.
I started housework, clumsily, noisily.
After an hour or so you stirred.

Then it began.

You were hot, you were restless,
you were tired,
you hadn't swallowed
all your many pills. I got them,
then got you up. I had to lift you,
you were so weak;
there was too much pain
in your back,
the cancers were breeding like bees.

3.
But slowly, staggering,
one hand leaning
over the other, both hands leaning on
the bathroom bench top,
you found your way
to the toilet.
I ran the shower, naked
to wash you,
then tore off the sweat-laden sheets
and scrapped new ones hurriedly
on the bed's corners.
You spent time on time
before you emerged,

hand over hand again, and made it
to the cleansing shower,
collapsed onto a stool.

You could soap your breasts
and I could your legs, but
on your back you had me just
squeeze soapy water –
all you could bear.
Out of the shower you shocked me:
I wanted to pat you dry
but you kept going
into freeze frame
and wouldn't have me
touch you, hunched over
like a crooked
backed statue.
I kept pulling towels out
to keep you warm,
and eventually got you back
to bed, all of three metres away.

An hour and a half shower
and after it
you just wanted to sleep.

4.
It was ages
before you let me ring a nurse
who was "busy", who promised
to come or ring, who in fact

would never ring
and never come. I kept
checking on you,
restless,
not sleeping.

It was dark before
you would let me
harangue the doctor,
the doctor we had seen six days before
when he tried to talk you into
perhaps attending our son's wedding
in Taipei. He was stunned
that I wanted you in hospital,
at first asking "Why?"
but conceded. At the bed I said
I thought I could get you there
but might need an ambulance.
Your head was nodding on the stalk
of your neck like a daffodil
as I struggled to get you,
flattened on the bed, unable
to move, to lift yourself,
onto a mobile chair, your
flip-flopping feet onto the frame
of the hospital-style table on castors.

5.
It took twenty minutes
to get you from bed to car;
you could take none of your slight weight

and my heart was pumping
a fast bongo beat by the time
I got you to the seat.
You've long needed a pillow behind
for the cancers in your back
but now you had a pillow
between the seatbelt and your stomach;
you looked like a human sandwich
upright because strapped
in place. We drove,
as fast as I could, you starting
occasionally into uncertain speech
but few words came out:

Saturday night, everyone getting out
in their glad rags, smiles on their faces,
the noise of fun starting to roar.

Saturday night, the hospital subdued
in semi-darkness, when I left you
slumped in the car, in five-minute parking,
and rushed to ask for a wheelchair
and a strong male nurse.
A receptionist surprised me:
I had to park at the door
to the new wing.
We waited. Minutes seemed
an agony of hours.

You were silent.

Eventually a wheelchair appeared, pushed
by a diminutive female nurse.
We nursed you into it, gradually,
and you were able
to help a bit.
The nurse took off immediately.

6.
By the time I found you, small
suitcase in hand, with clothes,
cardigan, medicines thrown inside
you were already in a buzz
of scurrying nurses, your arms
drip-fed. I could tell them about medicines
you needed and hadn't had. They
couldn't get a blood pressure,
the young nurse thought she was doing
something wrong, thought the machine
was kaput, but new machines
brought no readings.
You were moving in the bed, crying out
"Oh Christ!", "Oh Dennis!", until
painkillers pumped into a vein
gripped the pain a little. We all waited
for the doctor on duty
but I don't think you knew.
He came. He couldn't get a pressure.
I stayed, sitting in a chair beside you
but you were hardly aware. By 10
you had calmed into sleep

and I left, needing rest and food, and
normal human things outside
whatever dimension you were in.
I thought you would sleep through the night.
I'd been up since 5am
and my mind was sharply divided
between exhaustion and sharp,
shocked awareness, absolutely alert.
Back home I'd just finished
tasteless take-away pizza
when the phone rang – the nurse,
you were asking for me.
I threw pizza scraps and cardboard
aside, and rushed to the car
and the phone rang again,
the doctor this time. He wanted to know
if you should be kept alive
at any cost: I knew
this answer,
your emphatic "No!"
But he was just taking precautions,
considering just in case scenarios
as doctors must, almost
ultimate judges, on the brink
where few of us must ever go.

7.
Saturday night now in full swing.
When I reached the hospital
the doctor was already there,
asking you questions, and even
with eyes dumbly closed

you were answering.
He asked if you'd had the pain
all day, and you said "Pretty much",
sounding almost like you.
He and I looked at each other;
I could tell him about the day,
and he started to go through
possibilities: he was trying
to work out
what the hell had happened,
possibility one – No –
and then
it clicked: he knew
and I could tell that he knew.

You had slumped
into sleep but just then, with eyes
closed, called out weakly, "Dennis".

And he and I immediately stopped.
I think now
he moved back. I moved
to the head of the bed, and bent down
to you, said "Yes, My Love"
or some such, and you said, softly,
in drawn out, grasping, slow syllables,
"I need … to … go … home …
in … an ambulance".
I replied "Of course".

They were the last words you ever said.

Immediately you went back
to that nether world I could not enter.
I moved away,
asked him if we could
speak in the corridor:
 "She's not going to go home,
 is she?"
He said simply "No":
that blunt, final
wall of a syllable.
He explained
that your heart had bled
into the pericardial sac
around your heart. It was totally
unexpected. From there the heart
can't find the blood to pump
around your body:
that simple plumbing
we live by,
and you died by the heart
while I expected a race
between your lungs and your bowels.
Cancer had ambushed us yet again,
always a step ahead
of expectations, that bastard
of a disease. I was I think
in shock but strangely calm. Perhaps
I was so deep in sorrow
I could not tell what it was.
I asked him, "How long?"
but he wouldn't

dare guess. For some reason
"perhaps three days"
jumped into my head –
the period Christ took to rise
ingrained in Sunday School?

8.
I sent text messages, spoke a few times
to our older son, then settled
again beside your bed, a blanket
the nurses gave over me and the chair
and watched you breathing.
You slept calmly now.

9.
At 3am, a text in reply, and I spoke
to our younger son, who headed
for a plane. At 3.30 I thought
you would sleep through what was left
of the night, and so staggered home.

I did sleep, for perhaps an hour,
before the phone, that ominous instrument,
rang. I jerked upright,
looked at the clock – 5.40 – then
picked it up to a nurse's voice,
the voice who had rung hours before:
"I came into the room five minutes ago
and Rhonda stopped breathing". Shocked,
I said "Thank you". What do you say?
But I did mean it in some way

before I screamed at the empty,
empty house, let loose
a senseless burst of tears,
then shakily started the phone calls
to Sydney, three hours ahead,
the agonizing soft drama
of sending the unanswerable message of death.

I got to the hospital before
my cousin, and had these ten
precious minutes alone with you
in that peaceful room,
all tubes and machines gone, all nurses;
I was surrounded by silence
as I kissed you and told you
I loved you,
and always had
uselessly, as if that counted now
or you could hear.
You received me palely
and silently but looked
the most peaceful in years.
We sat with you for hours
until I let my cousin go. Each time
I thought to go
something pulled me down again.
We were both out of this world,
and yet when I looked
I saw the sheets move
below your increasingly ivory face:
above you the air conditioning
was breathing as if it were you.

It was eerie
and then somehow funny, as if
all the world's ironies had gathered
to this place
and these moments.

The blood draining
from your body, your lips purpling,
the longer I stayed
the less you looked like you.

10.
And so, eventually
I had to leave
and wandered out, drove out
into the aimless morning
in a mysterious world
but with the nurse's questions
about undertakers haggling
in my ears. I wondered
where to go
and all these months later
I still do.

ORANGES

The funeral service is over, the flowers have died
and the last, generous family visitors
have flown far away.
Only two cards today:
they're petering out.

Three weeks since you've gone
and I can barely believe it.
Time shrinks, evaporates like steam
or expands, yeast-like, and
I cannot take its measure. The calendar
is meaningless. You died yesterday
or ages ago, to me; sometimes
both, bizarrely, simultaneously.

It's not long since you bought oranges.
You thought in the haywire
system of your intestines
they would prevent "blockages".
Your doctor laughed.

The morning of your funeral
I washed my hair
with the last of your shampoo
as if to get part of you,
the smell of you, on me;
and now I toss the empty container
into the bin's mouth.

I visit family and friends,
who are kind
but getting on with their lives,
as they must. They don't see
a planet that
has stopped spinning
or me merely spectating,
adrift on a distant star.

It is finished.
All the suffering done, the long years of pain.
Yet the unsatisfiable monster of grief
heaves itself like a tortured animal.
What can I more honestly do
but take up an orange and bite?

ASHES AND HAIR

We have sent you to the great conflagration,
converted your unbelieving tongue to ashes.
We have incinerated your once lovely lips
and once strong bones, all your
once beautiful body
now compressed into a box.
I have a letter to prove it: your ashes
"can be collected anytime"
like some clipboard I've ordered.
Though you once
half-agreed to the fire,
guilt strokes my skin,
guilt fingers my mind,
guilt scorches my tongue.

I cleaned your brushes and was surprised
to find trapped in their snail-horn
knobbly feelers, scratchings
of your thin, grey,
once thick, brown hair,
that gathered into a small tuft.

Wills, certificates, accounts, cancellations
– there is so much to do
after a death,
some with things,
some inside the head.
I handle all
the bureaucracy and business

and in defiance
half-imagine you here.
Bright photo frames have you smile b.c.
– before cancer – as I clean through the house.
Cancer implores you to win
skirmishes but not the war.

I did try to care, and I failed.

You have gone to a better place some friends say,
there is a God, there is a Paradise, and you are there.
But nightly, as if to prove that you have died,
and what it means, you walk towards me
weirdly, made of ash, cinders
falling from your breasts, your eyebrows
and I am standing there, holding
thin scrags of your hair
like a talisman, terrified.

64A PRINCEDALE RD

Through the thudding underground
and its crouched, dusty stations, forty years on
I didn't really remember
the platform, or how you climb to the street
from the dark, and the name
"Holland Park Avenue" I had wrong
in my head, though you walked down it
so often, and I walked with you so often
all those years ago. The street I'm pretty sure
has changed completely, now more swish,
more flash, more contemporary
so, going solely on memory, no map
in my hand, I thought I must
have got it wrong, when suddenly
there was the name,

"Princedale Rd". Childishly thrilled,
I turned and walked along
towards the flat you once had,
my own Castle Boterel,
my step and heart quickening
until I reached 64a. I have a photo
of you seated in its window

and somehow, of all the photos
over all the years, it's these,
of you in London, young, full of hope,
full of adventure, the future
piling up in your pretty smile,

that razor wire my throat.
Somehow I can't credit
that it has all gone,
is sealed over now
in death, in all time's mystery
and menace, and I stood opposite the door
a pathetic figure in an ordinary street
on an ordinary day, if a sunny day
in London can be thought
ordinary, and tried to hold it all
in to me
uncontrollably.

NARVIK TWICE

There were few of us left
when the long overnight train
trekked at last into Narvik.
Above the Arctic Circle, I
stepped out into fragile,
delicate sunshine, the only one
not hunchbacked under a pack.

Forty-one years ago
we both humped one
and no-one else stepped down
into dark, furious blasts, the
winter air that seemed to gulp you in
and freeze your lungs.
Our journey had been fjords,
solid lakes, waterfalls
stopped in mid-sentence,
pines in snow overcoats
and ice sculpture birches
with sleet for leaves.
A customs officer – they had
such creatures then – rescued us,
drove to the youth hostel:
closed. Then to a guest house
warming to the only tourists in town.

The station is just the same,
I'm pretty sure, just as small
and inconsequential, with a walk up the hill

I do remember, now
I've come back alone.
Narvik is bigger no doubt
but still just a town:
there's nothing here
beyond memories
that make me
what I am. Some of them
I'm discovering again.

I walked the streets, and ate,
so little else to do.
For no-one there did I
have any meaning, nor they for me.
The next day summer was over,
the streets feted with rain.
You are dead. Why have I come?
A need to tell myself
that it is over, to seal
closed our love, our marriage
and all that it meant?
Sometimes now I reel
like a ghost in my own life.

I stood on Narvik's streets
with that increasingly familiar
concoction of satisfaction and pain,
adrift in Norway's drizzling rain.

GELATI ALLA SPIAGGIA
i.m. SD, GR and RH

We found it so bizarre, but still
loved it, as the brave photo I free
and hold and stare at proves:
Gustavo and Sheila, Rhonda and me

in overcoats, neck-scarved, upraised
gelati coloured in twos or threes, strolling
along the beach in our mid-winter
Rimini and Riccione trip. Something

in Italian life encourages the bizarre.
Today down Via dei Chiari I walked
past your old door, number 5: beside
the bell still sit your names, uncorked

from you: "Downing/Riboldi". My finger
lingered in the air, as if to stem the
uncertainty, ring and make you appear,
yet I realise your names condemn me

as the only one of us alive, *solo io.*
C'è la vita, what could be more clear?
But what of what we are could be
sadder, more shaking, and more bizarre?

GRIEF

Like a whale
with an arbitrary tale
grief can have you
tossed off the sea
in an instant of wild spray
as salt-drenched as tears.

Like a cat with a ball
of string, grief
can string you along
and just when you think
you're all right
show you you're wrong.

Like a coin tossed
into the sun
grief can have you spin
not knowing which side
you'll land, head
or tail
but inevitably
on edge.

"Death shall have no dominion"
one poet wrote,
and another,
"Death, thou shalt die!"
Grief will tell you
one was a joke
and the other a lie:

your emotions, your rationality, your ideas,
all are flimsy
faced with its seriousness, its
unimpeachable dramatic whimsy.

INSISTENCE

The dead have nothing to do with us.
It is only the living who inhabit
any dimension we can begin
to understand. Why then
do the dead determinedly
step through our sleep,
persistent zombies? Each night

I go to bed exhausted, and exhaustion
has me tossed for hours
in a roiling,
tumultuous sea; until blissfully
I sail into sleep –
then each dark
4am
you silently summon me;
telling me
that I understand nothing.
It is you.
But it is not you, and never will be.

Out on some broken reef of reality
waves rise, bank and crash,
each one an image of you,
all cancer gone,
thick, long hair and vivid smile,
your voice
voicelessly saying
you will not sleep.

I have so many promises to keep
and the horizonless sea
thrashes on forever,
your silent voice insisting:
You will
not sink. You will
not float. You will not sleep!

WIDOWER

"Widower". It's such an odd word
like something to do with threshing
or soaring: I caught this morning
morning's widower, stumbling down
wasted streets. It's against the odds:
women live longer than men,
wives than husbands. Everything about it
is wrong. Time with his clichéd scythe
has cut a vicious way.

And the words it sits with
have an odd ring, like
strangers in the house of our lives:
"ashes", "funeral", "loss", "death", "fire".
Can they ever exhaust their meanings,
tire of us and relax
their knuckle-laden fingers?

"Widower": this pathetic run
of weak, short syllables
says nothing about me
or everything, catching on
my every breath
the low, dark aftermath of death.

BIRTHDAY PRESENT
for Cameron

Meditation was a constant companion
when the roads led me down to
Margaret River's grape-swollen sunshine
for our son's birthday. I took with me
what I could tell him was
on the one hand just a shabby,
broken piece of plastic

and on the other was
the most important present
I would ever bring him:
the small, grubby wrist band
he had worn in hospital
when he was born
and that I found in his mother's purse
when emptying it out,

when I dared to clean out
all the sagging, split-seamed compartments
where she had nursed it
from the day she left hospital
carrying him, after he had lain
on each breast
and made his first grabs
at her fingers, her attention,
thirty-seven years before.

He was working thirteen hours a day
on vintage, and I marvelled
that his strong, young man's wrist
could have grown
from something so small
and that the miracle
of a mother's love
could outlive her
and all her treasured possessions.

FASCINATION

FASCINATION
for Livio Haskell

Five months into life
you have the utter helplessness
of the human, incapable
beyond any other animal.
Those hazel-tinged,
darkness-deep eyes
are totally open, mesmerised
by a twirling ceiling fan,
a swirl of clothes,
the screen-lit story
of Three Little Pigs
and their hapless wolf.

You suck on milk or whatever
vegetable or fruit mush
is proffered; food, sheets, toys
– everything goes
into your searching mouth.
You fling uncontrollable arms
at tables, people, discovering
what they do, amazed

when things cling
to your tiny, wild fingers.
The frothing ocean's sounds
slap into your ears.
You kick your legs
sideways, frog-like, forwards, whichways,

get your bottom dressed
without protest or helpfulness.

When tiredness overtakes
you curl into me
like a koala bear
into a tree
as if every leaf
were a sap-filled wonder,
as if I could
stand there forever.

ACKNOWLEDGEMENTS

Some of the poems were first published in *Acts of Defiance* (Salt Publishing, UK), *Asiatic* (Malaysia), *Axon*, *Indian Literature* (India), *Australian Love Poems 2013*, *Engaging with Literature of Commitment* (Rodopi, Amsterdam), *Indigo*, *Island Magazine*, *Journal of English Studies and Comparative Literature* (the Philippines), *Lines in the Sand* (FAWWA), *Salt Magazine* (UK), *Southerly*, *The Australian Literary Review*, *The Best Australian Poems 2014*, and *Westerly*.

"The Call" and "The Basis of All Knowledge" were first published in *Listening at Night* (Angus & Robertson, 1984); "No-one Ever Found You", "Tapping" and "Washing the Dishes" in *Abracadabra* (Fremantle Arts Centre Press, 1993); "Constancy" and "An Act of Defiance" in *All the Time in the World* (Salt Publishing, 2006). All of these poems were reproduced in *Acts of Defiance: New and Selected Poems* (Salt Publishing, 2010). My thanks go to these publishers for allowing republication here.

My thanks to friends who commented on drafts of some of these poems and especially to Isabela Banzon and Shirley Lim who read them all. I am very grateful to Wendy Jenkins and Georgia Richter at Fremantle Press for their thoughtfulness and sensitivity in helping to bring the original manuscript to its published form.

The line "an avenue, dark, nameless, without end" in "So Much Courage" is quoted from Edward Thomas.

CELEBRATING 40 YEARS OF UNIQUELY WESTERN AUSTRALIAN POETRY

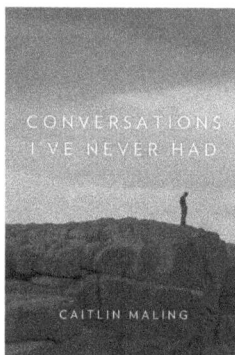

CONVERSATIONS I'VE NEVER HAD — CAITLIN MALING

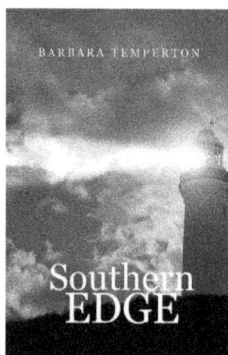

BARBARA TEMPERTON — Southern EDGE

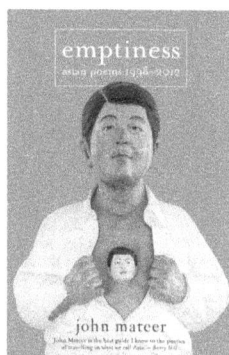

emptiness — john mateer

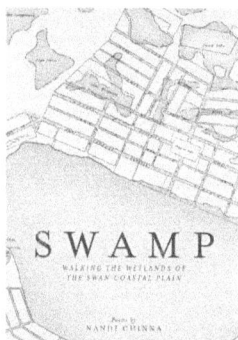

SWAMP — WALKING THE WETLANDS OF THE SWAN COASTAL PLAIN — Poems by NANDI CHINNA

sack — JOHN KINSELLA

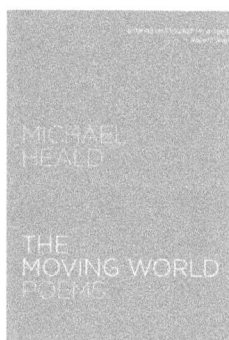

MICHAEL HEALD — THE MOVING WORLD POEMS

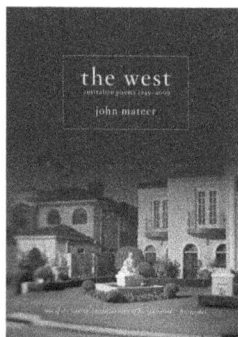

the west — john mateer

burning bright — caroline caddy

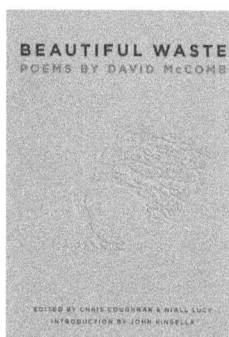

BEAUTIFUL WASTE — POEMS BY DAVID McCOMB — EDITED BY CHRIS COUGHRAN & NIALL LUCY — INTRODUCTION BY JOHN KINSELLA

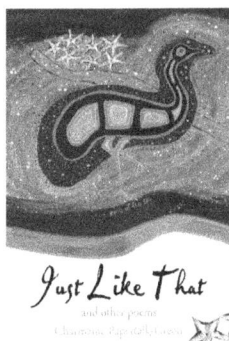

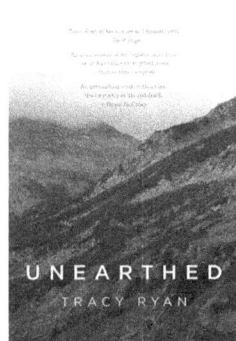

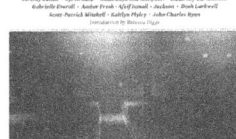

First published 2016 by
FREMANTLE PRESS
25 Quarry Street, Fremantle 6160
(PO Box 158, North Fremantle 6159)
Western Australia
www.fremantlepress.com.au

Cover design Carolyn Brown, furrylogic.com.au
Cover photograph courtesy of the author

A catalogue record for this
book is available from the
National Library of Australia

NATIONAL
LIBRARY
OF AUSTRALIA

ISBN: 9781925163285 (paperback)
ISBN: 9781925163858 (ebook)

GOVERNMENT OF
WESTERN AUSTRALIA | lotterywest

Fremantle Press is supported by the Western Australian State Government through the Department of Cultural Industries, Tourism and Sport.

Australian Government | Creative Australia

Publication of this title was assisted by the Commonwealth Government through Creative Australia, its arts funding and advisory body.